HOW ON EARTH CAN I BE ECO-FRIENDLY?

Written by Lianne Bell

Print information available on the last page.

Written by Lianne Bell
Edited by Allison Orr
Formatted by Lester Basubas
Cover design by Rebecca Strickson
Author photo by Gonzalo Bendito

Published by Lianne Bell
www.liannebell.com

"Everything starts with an idea."

**– Kate Tempest, Poet,
Playwright and Activist**

#howonearth

Foreword

The information in here is short, sharp and easy to digest. Thanks to technology, we all have the attention span of a goldfish, myself included.

This is a collection of my thoughts and moments in my life that have made me think about how I can be more eco-friendly in my day-to-day life. Some habits I've changed and some of them I'm still working on.

The book is divided into 3 sections which are imaginatively named Part I, II and III.

Contents

PART I... 12

#intro.. 13

#ootd 19

#sustainablefashion 38

#whomademyclothes 44

#wherewasitmade? 48

#whatisitmadefrom? 51

#makedoandmend 63

#shopsecondhand 67

#slowfashion 75

PART II 81

#foodgasm 82

#shoplocal 95

#reducereuserecycle 100

#zerowaste 107

#mealprep 111

#meatlessmondays 116

#plantpower 121

#growyourown 126

PART III 132

#selfcare 133

#skincare..138

#smellyalater 149

#safetyrazor 154

#periodpower...159

#bogroll..171

#EaudeBO 178

#bethechange 187

#educateandinspire.......................................195

References...204

"We don't need a handful of people living perfectly sustainable lives, we need millions of people doing it imperfectly."

– Anne Marie Bonneau. Blogger
aka @zerowastechef

#howonearth

PART I

#intro

Human beings are creatures of habit. Every one of those habits is something we have learnt from someone or somewhere. Living in an eco-friendly way doesn't have to mean sacrificing anything in your day-to-day life, or mean running into the nearest forest in your birthday suit to embrace a tree. It's simply about changing our habits. Nothing in this book is radical; it should all be easy enough. But, coming from someone who has had a penchant for cigarettes for more than half of their life, I know that habits are not always so easy to break. Even so, the first step is actually pretty simple, all we have to do is try….

Sustainable living* or anything associated with an organic lifestyle tends to be labelled as elitist. In this sense, having the financial security to make purchases on non-essential items does put us within the richest 6% on the planet. However, that doesn't mean we necessarily have huge amounts of disposable income.

 A trip to your local organic store to browse the insanely expensive vegetables or the fancy lotions and potions in the skincare section might leave you weak at the knees — even on the verge of a minor heart attack. The reality that most of us exist in day-to-day — yours, mine, and the working-class' — is that we are chalking off the days until the next payday. And when you're shopping on a shoestring, the last thing on your mind is whether or not your groceries are zero waste, or which country your socks were made in. That's what it's like for me anyway, and I know I'm not alone.

* Sustainable living: to live in a way that interacts positively with nature, while also avoiding the depletion of our natural resources.

But every time we use something once and throw it away, we're essentially throwing away our own money. Every time we make a repeat purchase on a product or buy something we don't actually need, the company we purchased from is laughing all the way to the bank with our hard-earned cash.

What if we could change that?

These are some of the ways I do things. I'm not rich, and as much as I aspire to, I can't fit my yearly waste into a jar. Sometimes I'm dairy-free for environmental reasons, but occasionally I devour a cheeseboard. Generally, I cycle everywhere, but sometimes I take an uber.

Being eco-friendly isn't about being perfect. It's about making small changes to your lifestyle -- changes so small that you'll barely even notice.

But if we *all* adopt these small changes...

...well, we might just be onto something.

"Remember that without change, there would be no butterflies. Without change, the dead of winter would never turn into the beauty of spring. Without change, the dark of night would never turn into the triumph of dawn."

– Jayda Skidmore, Author

#howonearth

#ootd

(#ootd which stands for outfit of the day, has just under 300 million posts of people sharing what they're wearing on that particular day. I'm more of an #outfitrepeater which trails behind with just over 33,000 posts.)

"Demand quality not just in the products you buy, but in the life of the person who made it."

– Orsola de Castro, Designer and Co-founder of Fashion Revolution

#howonearth

We have all known for years that our clothing is made using slave labour, and yet, by and large, we've done nothing.

Are we all evil sociopaths?

No, of course not.

In this case, the old saying 'out of sight out of mind' has never been more applicable.

Much like the unmeasurable amount of plastic pollution pouring into our oceans until we actually see something with our own eyes, it's hard for us to fathom.

That's just human nature.

145 people perished in the Triangle Shirtwaist Factory fire*. It was 1911 in New York City. There was only one functioning elevator in the factory, and only one fire exit that wasn't locked, one which, rather ominously, opened inwards. Owing to the fact that there was no way for anyone to get out, nearly no one did. Here in the 21st century, how is it possible that these kinds of hazardous working conditions still remain the reality for factory workers in the countries which make our clothing?

The health and safety records for overseas garment factories are mired with unsavoury situations. Examples include verbal abuse, withholding wages and passports, statutory pregnancy tests for female employees, and exposure to hazardous chemicals. Are these the kinds of issues we face in the workplace?

Hell no, so why should the people who make our clothes?

* the Triangle Shirtwaist Factory fire was the deadliest industrial disaster in the history of New York City. It paved the way for much more stringent workplace health and safety standards.

Bangladesh is the world's second-largest garment producer. The industry employs over four million people. Working in the garment industry is one of the only job choices available to uneducated women, resulting in this sector being the biggest employer of women in Bangladesh.

The country is also notorious for its lax health and safety standards; for example, many garment factories will lock their fire escapes. The reason cited for this is to avoid the workers stealing stock. However, the reality is that it's also to stop them from running away. As such, these factories are essentially death traps. On April 24th, 2013 in Dhaka, the capital city of Bangladesh, the Rana Plaza factory building collapsed.

Over 1,138 lives were lost that day, in what is now considered to be one of the worst industrial disasters of our generation.

It is commonplace for the factories in Bangladesh to add extra floors to the buildings without official planning permission. Oftentimes, buildings with foundations to support a two-storey building will end up as a four or five-storey building. This causes the building to be unstable and hazardous. In the worst-case scenario, such as Rana Plaza, the building may even collapse.

The unbelievable loss of life from this 2013 disaster at Rana Plaza reverberated across Bangladesh. People were left feeling numb, torn between the option of being able to provide a meal for their family and feeling safe in their place of work, something which we in the West often take for granted. Many of the people in these factories depend on their salaries to support many members of their families, like their children, their parents, or their in-laws. So, not only did many Bangladeshis lose their loved ones in the disaster, but they also lost their financial support too.

And whilst we are thinking about who makes our clothing, our insatiable thirst for cheap clothing and the subsequent ethical implications of this, we must also consider our environmental impact.

The rate at which we are consuming clothing is beyond nauseating, the number of garments being produced has doubled in the last 20 years.

We wear a garment an average of 4 times before it's replaced.

In fact, clothing is the only consumable which has deflated in price, completely defying the laws of economics...

But why has the price of clothing done a complete 180, dropping considerably in comparison to other consumables?

Well, when the Multi-Fibre Agreement* ended in 2005, this opened the door for suppliers and factory owners in developing countries to work on a larger scale with major corporations within the western retail world.

They were able to treat the labour of garment workers as though it were a commodity*. The factory owners offered labour at lower and lower prices to meet desired garment prices as demanded by the high street stores attempting to meet their profit margin targets.

Everyone's a winner...

...except for the people that are actually making our clothes.

* the multi-fibre agreement imposed quotas on clothing exports from developing countries to developed countries between 1974 and 2004.
* commodity - a raw material which can be bought or sold

If a skirt that cost £30 in 1994 costs £10 today, what's really so bad about that? If you're sat there wondering why cheap clothing is a problem, then do not fear, you are not alone. I thought the exact same thing.

The heart of the problem lies in the fact that we've come to think of clothing as disposable. However, clothing, as well as any other man-made items should not be thought of as disposable. This way of thinking diminishes all value and appreciation for the objects.

For example, how would you feel if someone gave you half a box of chocolates for your birthday? Whilst I'm not calling you ungrateful, I doubt many people would be jumping up to hug someone after receiving a dog-eared box of chocolates (with 5 of the best ones missing) as a birthday gift.

But the other day, that's exactly what I gave my friend for her birthday; she was over the moon.

But that's because, to most people,, everything in that box of chocolates is readily available.

It's the kind of chocolate people in Western countries see and eat all the time. But to those of us nestled 6000 miles away from the UK on an island in the Orient, this chocolate is comparable only to gold dust, or the Man Utd shiny if you're old enough to have had a premier league sticker book in 1995.

And because these particular chocolates are not instantly or readily available, they suddenly have a much higher value. Hence why my friend was so happy to receive them.

Therein lies the problem with the way we think about our clothing.

When something is so readily available to us, it devalues the whole item.

We don't even have to think about it; we just buy it.

We buy it aimlessly and needlessly.

Half the time, we'll buy clothing, then send it off to a charity shop without ever wearing it.

This creates a whole new problem. Once our high street charity shops are overrun by this kind of cheap, generic clothing, they bundle it off to developing countries where it is chopped up into rags, sold on at markets or thrown into a landfill.

The town of Panipat in North India recycles over 100,000 tonnes of our cast-offs every year. The women that shred these practically unworn garments have surmised that there is a water shortage in the Western world.

The mindless nature of our clothing consumption is so alien to them, that they assume it's too expensive for us to wash our clothes. This is the only way for some to make sense of how we discard clothing after only wearing it a handful of times.

Here is something worth considering: if we had to wade down our own streets through piles of our own discarded clothing, would we still be buying new clothes every week?

The mountainous problem of our discarded clothing remains very much out of sight, out of mind.

11 years ago, after a heavy weekend at Glastonbury Festival, my friends and I arrived back in the North of England.

I arrived at my parent's house at 9 am on Monday morning reeking of beer and regret and promptly hopped out of my friend's van and straight into my Dad's car. We then drove 60 miles South on the A1 to the city of Leeds where I was "studying" at University and spent the best part of a day moving house.

I think I must have had a moment of madness when I hatched that plan because I hadn't even finished packing. It was at this very moment, in my hazy, bewildered monster of a comedown, that I realised what a horrific number of clothes I had.

Worse still, I didn't even know what half of them were, I didn't even recall buying most of them and I had no recollection of ever wearing them either. But the worst part was when I noticed that half of them still had the price tags on.

If you want an example of mindless consumerism, there you have it.

I've racked my brain trying to figure out how I got to that point. I'd become a hoarder. A hoarder of cheap clothing.

Truth be told, although I've been strapped for cash for most of my life, I've still always had a fondness for expensive clothes. Even as a 10-year-old, I'd drag my Mum over to the Moschino section in the department store in Blackpool and give her palpitations when she saw the price of the jacket I was pawing with my grubby little skittles-stained mitts.

I think what I liked most about buying cheap clothing was that somewhere in my subconscious, it made me feel like I was rich. Growing up watching the likes of 'Clueless' with their endless shopping sprees and having my brain capillaries pummeled by TV ads, I was, as much as it pains me to say it, the quintessential Capitalist Kid.

So, it was there, aged 22, sat in a sleep-deprived state in the bedroom of my first student house with a two year Primark addiction under my belt, that I made the decision to end this ludicrous nonsense. I totaled up the cost of everything I'd purchased and realised that instead of spending £150 on a load of tat that I didn't even care about, I could have bought one really amazing designer piece in the sale that I would have probably worn to death and would still have today.

That was the moment when I decided to change my buying habits.

Now, when I see something I want to buy, I really consider the choice. I ask myself questions.

"Where will I wear it?" "What will I wear it with?" "How often will I wear it?"

I no longer buy items on impulse.

Much of the time, I'll leave the shop, go for a walk and think about it a bit more.

Does that sound like too much effort?

I take a break to weigh up the choice before I buy anything, a habit which formed as a result of becoming frustrated with myself for always buying pointless pieces of crap on autopilot. We all do it. We go and 'look' around the shops, and before we know it, we've bought a bag full of stuff that contributes to the clutter in our house. Then, we return home, never giving it a second thought again.

I've come out of this experience feeling like a brainwashed zombie in a warped utopia. And after watching Youtube videos of Black Friday shoppers, it's obvious to see that we are just about a mere whisker away from that very scenario.

After I've thought about a buying decision, I'll 'sleep on it'. According to most, this is what you should always do when making a decision.

The next day, if I decide that I still want to buy the item in question, happy to know that I'll wear it until it disintegrates in my bare hands, I'll go back and get it. I know I'm onto a good thing if I wake up in the morning and it's the first thing I think about. If I've completely forgotten about it, then it's clearly not worth my time.

And, yes, sometimes I go back for something to find that it's been sold, which leads to 15 minutes of heartbreak and devastation as I imagine all the fun we could have had together.

When was the last time you stopped and really thought about something before you bought it?

"We have to also change our mentality. It can't be that doing less bad is good."

– Gunter Pauli, Author and Entrepreneur.

#howonearth

#sustainablefashion

(searches for #sustainablefashion tripled between 2016 and 2019.)

"What if we started by slowing down and not consuming so much stuff, just because it's there and cheap and available. It's amazing how that process makes sense financially, it makes sense ethically, it makes sense environmentally."

– Andrew Morgan, Filmmaker and Director

#howonearth

Here's a question I've never understood: why must ethical and sustainable fashion have a special name?

Shouldn't these concepts be part of the normal way of doing things?

We want companies to use dyes that don't poison the people living around the factories.

We want companies to pay their workers a salary that will allow them to feed their families.

We want workers to have rights, such as holiday pay and maternity pay.

How can sustainable practice remain such a bizarre concept that it goes by a different name?

It's mind-boggling. And no, just because we might accept unethical, unsustainable sourcing to be the norm now, doesn't mean it has to be this way.

When I graduated from university back in 2011, there were only a handful of big names producing garments in a sustainable way who were showcasing them at Fashion Week.

And a lot of the time, the things that were shown at Fashion Week were so out-there that the wearer would have looked right at home drinking a cup of tea on the moon, but extremely out of place on the morning commute, which is what the majority of us are getting dressed for each day.

Bar a few big names, such as Katharine Hamnett and Stella McCartney, sustainable and ethical fashion just wasn't really a thing. It was mainly hemp trousers, hessian sack dresses, and coconut shell earrings. Not that there's anything wrong with them, but for sustainability to be fashionable enough to conquer the world, it needs to hit the zeitgeist.

Thankfully, over the last 10 years, interest in ethical and sustainable fashion has been on the up. In 2018, fashion search engine Lyst reported a 47% increase in shoppers looking for items with ethical credentials or certifications.

The way I see it, if we can control our lives on our phone, there is no reason we shouldn't be able to make trendy fabrics from environmentally friendly materials, or at the very least, make them out of materials we already have.

Over the last few years, we've seen the development of mock leather from pineapple leaves, soybean waste and mushrooms, thread from spider silk, along with athleisure and swimwear made with old recycled plastic, ocean debris, and even old coffee grounds. The future is on the horizon people and to be quite honest, it's looking rather fabulous.

"Becoming more mindful about clothing means looking at every fibre, at every seed and every dye and seeing how to make it better. We don't want sustainability to be our edge, we want it to be universal."

– Eileen Fisher, Fashion Designer

#howonearth

#whomademyclothes

(#whomademyclothes is part of a series of hashtags for the Fashion Revolution campaign. Fashion Revolution is an annual campaign to bring awareness to the exploitation within the fashion supply chain.)

It takes a CEO from a major fashion brand 4 days to earn the same amount that a Bangladeshi garment worker will earn in their entire lifetime.

Regardless of our job titles, we all work hard.

There is absolutely no excuse for why we cannot pay a decent living wage to the people that make our clothing.

The reason we don't…

is just pure unadulterated greed.

If you ask me what I hate most about the world we live in, it's exploitation and inequality.

It was this that piqued my interest in the ethics of fashion and the realization that my clothes were being made using slave labour. I just genuinely believed that was something we'd left behind in the last millennia.

I think it's an absolute travesty that we still face issues with slavery in 2020. There are an estimated 40 million slaves in the world at this very moment, and the majority of them are linked to the fashion industry.

I have long been a champion of ethical fashion amongst those that know me, meaning that sometimes, people send me messages asking questions about how to shop in a more ethical way. It also means that I sometimes find myself engaged in late-night debates on the topic.

A while ago I was chatting to a friend, who is a supplier based in London. We got onto the subject of child labour, as you do in East London, sat around a kitchen table at 4 am on a Sunday morning.

She was telling me how she had visited factories in India and Turkey, both of which had children working in them. By her reasoning, these children, around the ages of 9, 10 and 11, needed to work in the factories because they were responsible for helping to provide for their immediate and extended family members.

But I disagree with this. I feel that if their parents were paid a proper wage, then the children wouldn't be forced to work in the first place. The children would then have the opportunity to receive an education, resulting in them having better choices in life — something every human on this planet should be entitled to by birthright.

#wherewasitmade?

(Fashion Revolution uses this hashtag to bring awareness to the fact that as consumers we know very little, if anything, regarding the origin of the clothes we're wearing.)

If you cast your mind back, not too yonder in the past, the majority of our clothes were made in the UK. In fact, this wasn't just limited to clothing, the majority of the things we owned were all made in UK factories.

But towards the end of the 1980s, the allure of cheaper labour and increased profit margins for the big brands and retailers was too tempting and they moved most of their major production to the Far East, particularly China.

There is a common misconception amongst my friends that if they buy the top that's £85.00 as opposed to the top that's £3.99 then the people that made the more expensive top were paid a proper wage. This is not the case.

The price of the garment doesn't necessarily reflect the sum of money the workers are being paid. Lots of mid-range and designer diffusion lines are also manufacturing in countries with extremely low minimum wages using slave labour. It's not just the cheapest shops on the high street that are always the guilty parties.

If we want to start shopping sustainably one of the easiest things we can do as consumers is purchase clothing that is made locally to us. Etsy and Instagram are full of independent designers who are making and selling their own clothing from their home. This not only puts money back into the local economy but also results in a garment with a much lower carbon footprint than a comparable item bought from the high street.

#whatisitmadefrom?

(a report commissioned by Fashion Revolution found that 79% of people asked thought it was important for fashion brands to explain what their products are made from.)

"Without the oceans there would be no life on earth"

– Peter Benchley, Author,
Screenwriter, Activist

#howonearth

The most readily available natural fabrics on the mass market are cotton, linen, leather and wool. But just because they're natural doesn't mean they're environmentally-friendly. These fabrics are subjected to long, rigorous chemical processes before they reach our wardrobe.

However, the worst fabric eco-offender has to be polyester*. We use over 70 million barrels of oil every single year just to make polyester.

Just stop for a moment and think about what it takes to make that cheap polyester clothing: the very first step is extracting oil from the ground.

* polyester; a type of plastic used to make clothing, furnishings and other textiles.

Which muppet signed that off as a legitimate way for us to make our clothes?

The process of making polyester is tragic enough in itself. However, the real tragedy is the way that it's become commonplace to discard this garment after being worn a handful of times. Clothing made from polyester can take up to 200 years to decompose in a landfill.

With this reality in mind, we start to see that there is truly zero method behind this madness.

The majority of our clothes are made from a blend of polyester and a natural fibre such as cotton.

This clothing made from synthetic fabric releases microfibres.

Microfibres are the teeny tiny bits of plastic fibre that come off our clothing when they're in the washing machine. It's estimated that 30% of ocean plastic comes from microfibres. Europe coupled with Central Asia, are jointly responsible for dumping the equivalent of 54 plastic bags worth of microfibres per person, every week into the ocean.

The microfibres from our synthetically manufactured clothing not only pollute our oceans and beaches but, they're also ingested by fish, meaning that they eventually end up on our plates. We are essentially eating fish, chips, mushy peas with a side of old LBD* for our dinner. Yummy.

We've only very recently begun to understand the devastating effects of microfibres, and in all honesty, there's not a lot we can do at the moment.

You can buy a device like a guppyfriend* or cora ball* to wash your clothes in.

Or you can just wash your clothes less.

LBD is an acronym for little black dress.
Guppyfriend - a bag to wash your clothes in which collects microfibres.
Cora ball - a ball that goes into your washing machine to collect microfibres.

How much less you can get away with washing your clothes depends on the fabric. In 2014 Levi's CEO Chip Bergh confessed to CNN that his 10-year-old Levi jeans had never been in the washing machine, what a hero. But this is perhaps a tad unrealistic regarding your gym t-shirt, so be savvy.

Spot cleaning and airing your clothes were commonplace for our parents and grandparents generation but became less common practice for us thanks to the accessibility of the washing machine.

Reducing the number of times you wash your clothes saves water, reduces microfibers and it also prolongs the life of your clothes.

I like to think that the corporations which we buy our washing machines, clothing, food, toys etc from are working intently on creating systems that eliminate things like microfibres entering our oceans, reducing waste and manufacturing their products in a fair way.

But if the last few years have taught us anything, it's that we can't trust the imbeciles in charge.

Until the big guns catch on to this eco-friendly thing, we may need to help them to speed up the process.

People moan about social media all the time. And yes, we must face the facts, it is terribly addictive, but it's also rather wonderful.

Not so long ago, large corporations could and would hide behind their fancy logos and their endearing TV ads, and we'd believe every last word they said.

Those days are gone.

Thanks to the internet, not only do we see and hear more but we also all have a voice, a voice that can be loud and powerful, a voice that was once reserved for the educated echelons of the elite.

You can use social media to let your favourite brand know what you want them to do. I'm on the fence with regards to boycotting brands. It's true that we vote with our purse strings, but I want to see a change from the big brands. It won't happen overnight, but to start, you can DM your fave brand and tell them that you're bothered about this stuff. Recent trends in social media activism have shown us that they can and do listen. Taking action forces them to listen, especially when we're coming in droves.

Believe me, somewhere in that company will be a person using your messages as evidence to finance change within that company's supply chain
— so, get a wriggle on.

But if you want to do the easiest thing...

...the thing that requires zero knowledge and zero effort...

...the thing you can start doing this very second...

...and if you don't want to have to ask yourself a load of questions whilst you admire that jazzy shirt idly swinging on the hanger...

...there is a solution.

It's something that seems so simple, yet something we all struggle with.

Stop buying stuff.

"Raising awareness on the most pressing environmental issues of our time is more important than ever"

– Leonardo Dicaprio, Actor and Activist

#howonearth

#makedoandmend

(with almost 75,000 posts this movement is on the up recently as millenials revert back to mending something as opposed to replacing it with something new.)

"As consumers we have so much power to change the world by just being careful in what we buy."

– Emma Watson, Actress

#howonearth

I love the make do and mend movement, even though I still can't sew for shit.

My Instagram is full of patchwork denim, darned socks that resemble rainbows and sparkly embellishments covering rips, tears, and holes.

Backtracking to what I was saying earlier about the monetary value of clothing cheapening it in every sense, here is a great example of my point. Somewhere between the cassette dying and the CD taking off, we stopped mending our clothes. I'm sure there's a number of socio-economic factors that have contributed to this, but, generally speaking, who honestly wants to sit down and mend something when it only costs £10 to replace?

It's much easier to just buy a new one. So, that's what we do.

Meanwhile, none of us are considering the amount of resources it takes to make that piece of clothing that we can't be bothered to mend.

Take something simple, like a tshirt, for example. It takes around 2,700 litres of water to make a single t-shirt, just one. Think how many t-shirts you've owned in your life so far.

2,700 litres is roughly the same amount of water that the average person consumes in 2 and a half years.

We only have to take a look at the world's dire water-shortage situations, such as the major droughts in California, or the barren Aral Sea* in Uzbekistan, to know that water is not something we can ever take for granted, and yet we do.

* the Aral Sea was once the world's fourth largest lake and has now almost completely dried up after the water was diverted to irrigate the cotton crop in Uzbekistan.

#shopsecondhand

(the resale market is expected to outperform the fast fashion sector within the next 5 years.)

"I exclusively buy used clothes… I'm going to be a citizen of this planet, and I'm going to do my responsibility and live in stride with nature instead of constantly fighting against her."

– Shailene Woodley, Actress

#howonearth

During my aforementioned traumatic house move post-Glasto, I had a eureka moment.

Instead of spending 15 quid* on something from Primark, I could buy some secondhand Levi's shorts from my local vintage store. In fact, I could buy them for the exact same price as a cheap pair of Primark shorts.

That pair of Levi's shorts would last me an eternity.

It was then that it dawned on me, that buying secondhand is one of the simplest and easiest ways to shop sustainably without needing a fountain of sustainability know-how under your belt.

* quid; a british slang word for pound (GBP)

Apparently I'm not the only one to cotton onto this. A recent report by 'thredup' the world's largest online thrift store found that resale has grown 21 times faster than the apparel market in the last 5 years.

As the old saying goes, "one person's trash is another person's treasure." I live by this motto. Maybe I need to get out more, but honestly, nothing brings me greater joy than finding an absolute gem in a charity shop or at a jumble sale.

One of my fave tops at the moment is an M&S velvet vest top I got 6 years ago from a charity shop in London for the worldly sum of £3.00.

And, one of my all-time fave dresses was found in a bin. No joke. Circa 2010, I was walking through Hackney in East London with a can of K cider in my hand and a spring in my step, when I stumbled upon a bin bursting with handmade clothes. Jackpot.

One of the items was a little dress; it was the coolest thing I'd ever seen, even if it was a touch too small for me.

It was a bandeau style, with ruffles around the bottom made from pink floral fabric, and the top was a nude-coloured netting which formed the part around the shoulders. It was when that deceptive style had just come out. So, at first glance, it looked like the top bit of the dress wasn't there. It was half-finished, still with pins around the hem and in the ruffles.

As I've already clarified, I'm tragic at sewing, so I just wore it with the pins in. Sometimes I'd be out having a boogie, and one of the pins would suddenly prick my thigh. It was a stark reminder that nothing in life ever comes for free.

I don't know if it's a Northern thing, or if it's just the area where I grew up, but I remember the stigma attached to secondhand shopping when I was at school. There was a ridiculous social stigma attached to buying secondhand. A few years ago, I was in Blackpool visiting my cousin when I saw a little charity shop. My eyes lit up like the illuminations that Blackpool is so famous for, because, and if you've been to Blackpool you'll know, it is jam-packed full of old people. My Auntie calls it 'god's waiting gate'. Old people equal fashion-related treasure, from at least the 1980s, maybe even the 1960s if you're lucky.

Suffice to say, my cousin had a small meltdown as I motioned for us to step inside. She was around 13 at the time, and clearly I'd forgotten what it was like to be a teenager. I'd nosedived like a ravenous seagull from the cool older cousin to a social has-been. She insisted on waiting for me across the road.

"When you wear vintage, you never have to worry about showing up in the same dress as someone else."

– Jessica Alba, Actress, Author and Entrepreneur

#howonearth

#slowfashion

(slow fashion is the antichrist to fast fashion. A term adopted
by ethical fashion businesses with a slower business model
and those shopping in a more sustainable way.)

When you factor in the resources used to make our clothing, the intensive manufacturing process and the volume at which we consume clothing, it's clear to see that we simply cannot sustain this.

I first came across the term 'fast fashion' whilst writing my dissertation back in 2011. 'Fast fashion' is a term that was coined to describe the way in which Zara produces clothing. Whereas traditional high street fashion up until the 1990s had changed seasonally, changes in technology meant the way we consumed clothing could be sped up. Suddenly, instead of stock rotating every few months, it was changed out every few weeks.

To paraphrase Oscar Wilde, "fashion is a form of ugliness so intolerable we must alter it every 6 months." But how ugly does it have to get to necessitate altering it every 6 weeks?

In the last 3 years, I've bought fewer than 20 pieces of new clothing.

Despite my knowledge on sustainable fashion, I don't own that many sustainable brands.

My way of shopping sustainably is to only buy the things I need.

When I do buy something, it's normally something I can wear until either its, or my own, eventual death.

My most recent purchase, a denim skirt, was the equivalent of £95. I fully intend to wear it at least once a week until I draw my pension or it falls apart, except (fingers crossed) denim shouldn't ever fall apart.

A friend recently commented on the fact that I was wearing the same denim skirt she'd seen me in the week before, then made a backhanded comment about me "really getting my wear out of it".

It's this kind of attitude that needs to go.

Why can't we celebrate our wears? Instead, we have this cloud of disgrace hovering above the number of times we've worn something.

It has been indoctrinated into us.

I've been receiving comments like that for years. Back in 2014, I tried to explain my stance on clothing consumption to a work colleague after he commented on the fact I wore my £50 leggings, which were ethically manufactured in Australia, "way too much".

At £50 a pop, I couldn't stretch as far as buying 5 pairs, so I settled on 2 pairs. They were unique, and thus very obvious when I alternated between them. I honestly don't see what the big deal is with this. Either that or I just don't give a flying fudge. I think our attitudes towards re-wearing clothing come back to the fact that having lots of clothes makes us feel rich, and wearing the same thing all the time makes us worry we'll look poor.

We seem to have forgotten that less is more.

"We (consumers) have the power....we are in charge."

– Livia Firth. Co-founder of Eco-Age

#howonearth

PART II

#foodgasm

(there are 52 million pictures of food on Instagram just under that hashtag. WTF is wrong with us!?)

"Globally, around 1.3 billion tonnes of food are wasted every year."

– Jenny Gustavsson, Research Scientist

#howonearth

The production of our food creates greenhouse gases* along the entire supply chain. So, if we waste that food, not only are we wasting our resources, but these greenhouses gases have also been produced in vain.

The UK alone wastes around 10 million tonnes of food and drink every single year. Globally, wasted food is around 1.3 billion tonnes. Over half of this amount, roughly 60%, could be avoided going to waste. This food waste has profoundly negative impacts on the environment as well as the economy.

And, for this "little" problem, we have the supermarkets to thank. They are indeed both a blessing and a curse.

* greenhouse gas; a gas that contributes to the greenhouse effect. Carbon Dioxide, Methane, Nitrous Oxide are three main greenhouses gases.
(greenhouse effect; radiation from the atmosphere warms the planet because the heat from the sun cannot be released)

The one-stop supermarket shop and ready-meals, along with the invention of marvellous contraptions, such as the hoover, have all played a huge part in the rising number of women in the workplace. The advent of things such as these has allowed today's women to manage both the home and a career, something which wasn't a viable option for the majority of our grandparents. But these huge supermarket conglomerates, whose sole purpose it is to make money, have a lot to answer for.

I'm going to use Tesco as my example. This is purely based on the fact that they have the biggest market share in the UK, and also because I developed a strange obsession with them when I was 20 and read three books on the company.

(It was a slightly healthier obsession than the psychedelic effects of fungi, which arrived shortly after.)

There is rather famously only one town in the whole of the United Kingdom which doesn't have a Tesco: a small North Yorkshire market town with the revolutionary spirit to match the whole of France called Harrogate.

If you're wondering why the number of Tesco supermarkets is remotely relevant to this book about being eco-friendly, the fact is, and this is probably quite a bold statement, but I've got red hair, so I'm just going to say it: supermarkets are dicks. Yet, we all shop at them, myself included. But there are many reasons why we shouldn't.

The area where my parents live, and where I spent my teenage years is a relatively new suburb in the North East of England, an area with poorly-planned infrastructure with thousands of people using the same main road every morning to travel into the closest town to get to work. The traffic is a well-known joke in the area, and I'm pretty sure there's even one bottleneck junction with its own Facebook group. It's an area bordered by greenbelt land and woodland, with bike paths adjacent to the road and kids playing with their friends. With such severe traffic problems, an application by the local Tesco to extend to a superstore was rejected, quite rightly so, on the grounds of the lack of infrastructure. But did Tesco slope off quietly into the corner with its tail between its legs? No, it offered the local council to pay to build a dual carriageway on the road leading up to Tesco and their offer was duly accepted and the planning permission was granted.

This would have meant increased traffic and noise pollution in a residential area, something which we should be striving to decrease, not increase. There are a significant number of traffic studies which conclude that building bigger roads only creates more traffic. So, whilst expanding roads would appease the residents, in the long term it would only make the problem much worse.

This is just one example of a store that has shunned the considerations of the local environment for their own gain. We have almost 90,000 supermarkets in the UK. How often does this kind of situation take place?

And then, we see the waste that's generated by supermarkets. A bigger store equals a bigger volume of waste. With humongous volumes of packaging waste, not to mention the food that supermarkets put in the bin, it's a sight that would make your eyes water.

My very first job some 17 years ago was working as a sales cashier at my local Safeway, which now houses the aforementioned Tesco. I used to scan groceries for 9 hours every week in exchange for £30, and I can still vividly recall my horror when I discovered the trollies piled with food, that were making their way to the bin at the back of the supermarket.

I was genuinely shell-shocked. I just never thought that a tin of unsold chocolates would be thrown into the ground, especially when someone somewhere would gladly eat them. There's nothing that hurts my heart more than seeing something perfectly useful being buried in the ground. It just doesn't make any sense to me.

Supermarkets are not just wasting unsold food, they are also culpable for the insurmountable volume of food that is wasted before it even makes it to the store. In 2015, critically acclaimed TV chef, Hugh Fearnley-Whittingstall, in cahoots with Channel 4, brought it to the attention of the British public just what the supermarkets were truly capable of.

Somewhere along the line, it had been denounced that vegetables must be more aesthetically pleasing than something that you're willing to date at the age of 29. The result is hundreds of tons of vegetables being rendered 'unsellable' and thrown on the scrap heap before they've even made it to the supermarket shelves.

If and when an item does eventually make its way to the supermarket shelves, it's shrouded in the skin of commerce* and shrink wrapped to within an inch of its life before being forced upon us using psychological manipulation, not too dissimilar to the fashion industry. I understand this sounds slightly melodramatic for a statement on the weekly food shop, but bear with me on this. Every single thing in the supermarket is strategically placed for maximum sales, and maybe I'm naive, but I was surprised when I learnt this.

I didn't realise there was so much psychology behind these supermarket set-ups, used purely for the sake of making us want to buy things we don't need. Bread is always at the back; that's because you only go in for a loaf of bread, but then you have to walk past everything else. And those bars of chocolate that they sneakily place on the shelves separating the queues are certainly not there by accident.

* the skin of commerce also known as plastic film or cling film.

You need to have some serious willpower to enter a supermarket.

A trip to Tesco makes getting through the Tough Mudder* look like getting a pedicure.

My Dad would visibly shiver in horror when my Mum declared that she was "popping" to the supermarket for some bits.

An hour later, and with a receipt displaying the spine-shivering sum of £102.00, she would return and proceed to stock up the cupboards until they resembled a bunker preparing for World War III.

* Tough Mudder is an obstacle course endurance event

And that's because she'd fallen hook, line, and sinker for every mind trick that the supermarket has mapped out for her. She'd spent money she didn't need to spend and bought a trolley full of stuff she didn't need to buy. The majority of the population is just like my Mum.

For too many years, we've been duped into buying items we don't need on the premise that it is saving us money. A study by the Money Advice Service* found that we are spending an extra £1000 every single year because of these so-called deals.

The message is surely clear: just buy what you need.

* the Money Advice Service is the largest provider of debt advice in the UK.

"It's coming home to roost over the next 50 years or so. It's not just climate change; it's sheer space, places to grow food for this enormous horde. Either we limit our population growth or the natural world will do it for us, and the natural world is doing it for us right now."

– David Attenborough, Broadcaster, Presenter and Natural Historian.

#howonearth

#shoplocal

(I don't know about you but I hate the thought of my hard earned dosh going into the bank account of some pompous twerp sat on his jacksy on a yacht in the Cayman Islands.)

I saw a picture of a sandwich board on Instagram recently that says when you shop at a local business your money is being used to buy their child a school uniform or to pay their mortgage.

It's so obvious, but actually I'd never thought of it like that before.

My bank balance is a testament to the fact that I am no economist. However, what I recently realised is that for communities to thrive we must think of our dosh going in a circular motion. If anyone tries to tell you that money trickles down*, the chances are they're over 50 and have a considerable amount of cash in an offshore investment fund.

* *trickle-down theory: when benefits for the wealthy trickle down to everyone else and stimulate economic growth.*

And where does our money go when we shop at a large corporation?

Well, a portion of it is going towards the jobs they provide in the local area, there is no mistake in that.

But a large chunk of it goes to shareholders*. And, as if to add insult to injury, a lot of these large companies avoid paying the correct amount of tax, too.

So why do we even bother to shop at supermarkets? Well, they're convenient. And, as I mentioned earlier, this convenience has allowed us humans, and particularly women, to pursue the careers, hobbies, and interests that we are passionate about.

* shareholders: people with shares and financial investment in a company.

What it boils down to is that we're all busy.

In our spare time, we want to be able to enjoy ourselves. Whichever way you look at it, shopping for a few carrots and a bird for the Sunday dinner isn't exactly fun. We want to buy those things as quickly as possible so we can get down the boozer* with our mates or go home to do a jigsaw puzzle with the kids.

But this book is about changing habits, and the thought of shopping at the local market, like other changes, only seems inconvenient now because it means changing your routine.

* the boozer is an English slang word for an establishment selling alcoholic beverages.

So, like with everything, start off small; shop at the local market once a month and build it up until you're doing it on a regular basis. There will always be the night you finish work at an ungodly hour and nip into the local supermarket, feeling like a deflated balloon, to buy a ready-made meal wrapped in plastic. We've all been there.

Do not feel guilty about this. We'll never get anywhere if we're riddled with guilt or crippled with anxiety about how much there is to do and how little we're doing.

As long as we're trying, that's all that matters.

#reducereuserecycle

(the 3 R's has over 1 million posts. We've been using recycling as our primary option to be more sustainable but actually it should be the last port of call.)

"Waste isn't waste until we waste it."

– Will.I.Am, Musician

#howonearth

At this moment in time, the UK doesn't have the technological infrastructure to deal with the amount of plastic waste we're generating.

We've been shipping it off to other countries to deal with. Countries such as China, the Philippines, and Malaysia.

 And in 2018, China turned around and gave us the V's*. They closed the doors; they said no more. Fair play to China, as they've potentially done us a favour.

Because now, we've finally woken up to the mess we've been making.

the V's or the V sign is a hand gesture with the palm facing and the middle and index finger raised. It has been an insult in commonwealth countries for over one hundred years.

I always justify my consumption, probably like most people, with the fact that whatever waste I'm creating is recycled, and therefore it's ok.

But it's only when you delve into the murky world of recycling, (yes, my life really is that exciting) that you truly realise what an absolute pickle we're in.

Over the last couple of years, thanks in part to shows such as Blue Planet II, we've seen a reduction in plastics-use due to the Attenborough effect*. We've gotten closer to understanding the true extent of our plastic consumption. This unsustainable behavior is already resulting in devastating environmental consequences.

In particular, our oceans, coastlines and the animals that call those habitats their homes have been impacted by overconsumption of plastic.

* a reduction in single-use plastics named after all-round legend, David Attenborough.

It was in 2016, whilst travelling in India, that I had a stark realisation about plastic consumption. At that point, I still hadn't yet realised just how much plastic I had in my everyday life; I'd never stopped and thought about it. It was only when I actually saw how many plastic water bottles I'd consumed in a matter of days that it really hit me. I assumed, quite wrongly of course, that the plastic I used in London was recycled, but when I saw the cows chowing down on old plastic bottles as I hurtled down the winding lanes of Pushkar*, and the piles of discarded plastic in the streets of Jaipur*, that I truly realised what an ugly epidemic it was. Because for the first time in my life, I could see it with my own eyes.

When I was in London, though I didn't see the actual piles of waste I was personally generating, that doesn't mean they weren't there.

Jaipur; the capital city of Rajasthan state in India.
Pushkar; a town bordering the Thar Desert in North East Rajasthan.

Plastic in its current form can only be recycled a handful of times. PET plastic, which is the plastic most commonly used for food and beverage packaging, is only recyclable once or twice before it's off into landfills.

Just stop and look around at all the plastic you can see right now: your phone case, tubs of face cream, bottles of stuff to clean the kitchen, kids toys, plant pots, your kettle, your crisp packet, that little table on the train. It's everywhere.

Since plastic's conception some 60 years ago, it's estimated that we've created 8.3 billion metric tons of it.

And pretty much every single piece of that plastic is still lurking somewhere on our planet.

If it can't be reduced, reused, repaired, rebuilt, refurbished, refinished, resold, recycled or composted, then it should be restricted, designed or removed from production.

– Pete Seeger, Folk Singer

#howonearth

#zerowaste

(It's become a bit of a buzzword lately and it has 5 million posts to prove it. It's an Interesting concept although none of us can ever truly be zero waste.)

Last spring, I went to a techno festival on the beach. Besides being absolutely banging, it was also my first festival since I had started trying to reduce my consumption of single-use plastics some 18 months before. I have a mason jar with a handle and a hole for a straw in the top of the lid. We'll call it a 'jup', as it's neither jar nor cup.

I used this for my coffee, my gin and tonics and also my water when I lost my water bottle. And at the end of the festival, as I dragged my broken, sunburnt body from my flooded tent, which was now masquerading as a sauna, I noticed everyone carrying a huge bin bag full of rubbish from their tents. I looked down at my total waste for the 3 days, I'd amassed 2 paper plates, 1 paper box, 1 plastic water bottle and a couple of handfuls of cigarette ends which I'd been putting in my coat pocket because I'm not capable of using a portable ashtray when I'm wasted.

I don't want to blow my own trumpet, but I'm going to anyway because I was mightily impressed with my effort. So, if anyone has a spare Blue Peter badge* lying around, I'm eagerly awaiting it in the post. Because in all honesty, I hadn't even really tried. I'd barely made any effort. All I did was take my 'jup' and my water bottle and from doing that, I'd saved a whole bin bag full of rubbish. Imagine if everyone at the festival had done this. It's likely that there'd hardly be any waste at all. And as human beings with consciousness, is it not our duty to engage our brain a little bit? Even if we are a bit worse for wear.

It's taken me 14 months to get into the habit of taking my containers with me when I go out. My 'leaving the house' checklist is now phone, keys, purse and Tupperware. I had a little sign by the front door to remind me for at least 6 months and I still used to forget all the time. But now that I've gotten into the habit of it, it's just second nature.

* an award in recognition of achievement issued by the BBC children's programme; Blue Peter.

An added bonus to taking your own container is the discount on food and drink, although the saving isn't enough for me to save for a deposit on a house. I'd have to sacrifice my avocados for that, but it's better than a kick in the teeth.

As my Granny used to say, "Pennies make pounds." In this context, I could understand the reluctance of being eco-friendly if it was going to cost us more money. But often, it can save us money.

Find me one person that doesn't want to save themselves a few quid here and there. It's impossible.

This is where our love of the bargain originated from in the first place. But sometimes we forget that it's only a bargain if we're receiving a discount on something we are actually going to use. A lot of the time we buy things just because it's cheap, and we are not the winners in that equation.

#mealprep

(according to Instagram there are already millions of people preparing their meals. Many of these do it for health reasons, many of them probably do it for the gram but it's also the easiest way to reduce food waste too.)

If the term 'meal prep' conjures up images of crossfitters*
weighing their macros and carefully spooning out their carbs
into Tupperware containers, then you're not alone. But the act of
sitting down each week, planning what you're going to eat and
creating your shopping list from that not only saves you time and
money, it'll help save the planet too.

I talked earlier about those shops we all know and love;
the supermarkets. How many times have you been into a
supermarket and seen a 'buy one get one free' offer? You feel
like you've got a great deal because now you have two even
though you're only paying for one. Fast forward 7 days and the
extra one the supermarket gave you has gone mouldy, ends up
in the bin and contributes to the millions of tonnes of food waste
that we generate every year.

* Crossfitter: a member of high-intensity fitness program, CrossFit.

I can't be the only person whose Grandma would throw the previous nights leftovers in a frying pan to make bubble and squeak?

But many in our generation have gotten a bit complacent with regards to food and seem to have no qualms about wasting it. The ubiquitous BOGOF offer has been a contributing factor, as has the confusion surrounding the 'best before date' and 'sell-by date'.

I was never one to follow those dates on food, to be honest, I couldn't afford to. If it wasn't mouldy, I ate it, though obviously not things like chicken, or eggs.

I remember at university, one of my housemates had thrown away six pork pies with a best before date for the date of that day. We all now know that the best before date is related to quality, not safety. But in 2006, this little fact eluded us.

Never one to pass up a free meal, I fished them out of the bin. They were still in their plastic wrapper, completely unopened.

I shared them with my other housemate who was absolutely ecstatic since neither of us could afford anything as fancy as a pork pie.

And there we sat on the sofa, watching reruns of Hollyoaks, gorging on pork pies I'd found amongst the rubbish.
The true definition of living the dream.

Did we get the runs? vomit uncontrollably? Turn green and grow two heads?

No. We lived to tell the tale.

But how many people in the UK today are wasting food like this?

"In a world of seven billion people, set to grow to nine billion by 2050, wasting food makes no sense."

– Achim Steiner, UN Under-Secretary-General and UNEP Executive Director

#howonearth

#meatlessmondays

(Meatless Mondays originated in World War II as a method of food rationing. It was revived over 50 years later to combat excessive food consumption, the exact opposite reason it was originally coined for.)

The term Meatless Mondays was first coined in the States back in 2003 as a campaign initiative to improve the health of Americans and the planet. Over the last 16 years, it has grown into a globally recognised movement.

Eliminating meat one day a week in exchange for a day of vegetarian meals is something we can all do. It's a great way to begin the shift towards a more plant-based diet and the positive impact on the environment from this is pretty staggering.

Because, regardless of where you stand on the ethics of eating animals, you cannot deny the environmental implications of our food chain.

And there lies the problem: the chain.

It's the way we consume meat that's the problem.

Traditionally we slaughtered our own animals and consumed meat slowly and on special occasions.

But over time, our way of life has changed. Like many things, we've demanded more and our reliance and expectation on meat is putting an unnecessary strain on our resources.

Global food production accounts for somewhere between one-quarter and one-third of all man-made greenhouse gas emissions with the majority of that from the livestock industry.

Indeed, cows, as well as tasting mighty fine on a BBQ, are particularly horrific for the planet. One cow can produce up to 120kg of methane per year.

Methane is 23 times more environmentally damaging than CO_2. Methane emissions' total impact on the greenhouse effect is almost a third as much as carbon dioxide.

Our expanding population requires an expanding number of animals to feed that population. As of 2012 we are maintaining 60 billion animals to provide our meat, dairy, eggs and leather. These are living, breathing things which require an astronomical amount of food and water.

"If we gave up eating beef we would have roughly 20 to 30 times more land for food than we have now"

– James Lovelock. Scientist, Environmentalist, Futurist

#howonearth

#plantpower

*(If you need some inspo for eating more plants it'll be here.
3.5 million pictures of dribble inducing plant-based meals.)*

Flexitarian:

A person following a semi-plant based diet, less restricting when compared to traditional diets.

"Sandra doesn't eat meat on Mondays. She is a vegan on Tuesday, Wednesday, and Thursday and for the other 3 days of the week she eats whatever the fuck she wants."

Up until very recently, there was no question of my Dad eating a vegetarian* or vegan* meal. Even if I sneakily made him a plant-based meal, he would refuse to eat it and claim he wasn't hungry as soon as he discovered the absence of meat.

After talking to my friends I know my Dad is not the only Dad to do this. And I'm sure it will come as no surprise that men in his age group are the biggest consumers of red meat. Big Poppa B would eat red meat every day without hesitation if he could.

* vegetarian meal: food which doesn't contain any meat.
* vegan meal: food which does not contain any animal products whatsoever, including meat, dairy or eggs, and sometimes honey.

Due to my incessant nagging over his acceleration in age and his increase in cholesterol, eventually, my Mum began to slyly cut down on his intake of red meat. And began "quietly" moving him towards a more plant-based diet, and recently even fully vegan items.

If you'd told me this a few years ago you could have blown me down with a feather. But thanks, in part, to my Mum's fabulous culinary skills, my Dad had been unable to tell that the meatballs and lasagne he had been devouring every week were in fact made entirely of plants.

I had been quietly relishing this fact over in smugsville for a good 6 months before she finally let the cat out the bag. I'm very proud to say that they now only eat red meat twice a month.

And the point to this long rambling tale is that if my Dad, who is basically allergic to change and all things new, can change his diet and reduce his red meat consumption by 83%, then anyone can. Even just by reducing your intake of red meat by 50%, you can cut your carbon footprint in half.

Reducing our meat consumption is vital because from an environmental perspective, as I've already highlighted, we just don't have the resources required to farm the amount of meat we're consuming. It's just not sustainable.

The deforestation, the food waste, the greenhouse gas emissions... when you take a step back and look at the bigger picture, it dawns on you how utterly impossible it all is.

#growyourown

(It's only in the last 50 years that we've stopped growing our own food as the convenience store and the supermarket have taken off.)

Back in 2005, I was in my first year of university. Along with my brand new housemate Suzie, who is now one of my dearest friends, I pledged to master the art of cooking over the ensuing months. When I first arrived at university I invited my new group of friends over for dinner and presented them with plates of turkey dinosaurs and potato waffles. So, trust me, I had my work cut out. Thankfully, I discovered the power of a wok and the rest is history.

And as we slithered into our second year of study, we moved into a house with a garden and duly pledged to master the art of gardening by growing all of our own vegetables.

That never happened, the only thing we mastered was the art of the 24-hour bender.

15 years later writing this, and I still haven't gotten to grips with gardening. I always blame this lack of skill on the fact I live in a city. The city where I currently live has a population of 3.5 million and is on an island sandwiched between Japan and the Philippines, nestled snugly on the Pacific ring of fire. It's also home to the world's biggest coal plant which doesn't exactly fill me with enthusiasm for growing tomatoes on my balcony.

But like the rose that grew from concrete, urban farming is a thing, and it's blossoming. Balcony gardens, rooftops, and allotments are all popular ways to grow your own veggies in the middle of the city. Aside from being one of the best things to do for your bank account, growing your own food is also one of the easiest ways to disrupt the system and take back some power from the big conglomerates.

I have never been to Detroit, Michigan. In fact, I've never been to the US. But even so, I know that I love Detroit.

We can all learn a thing or two from the people of Detroit. It's as though they saw us English folk piddling around on our allotments and, in true American fashion, thought to themselves, "We'll have a go at that, but we'll do it ten times bigger."

Agrihoods are the integration of agriculture into residential areas. They provide recreation for members of the community in addition to much-needed fruit and vegetables. These vital resources are offered at an accessible price point so that they're available to everyone, regardless of their financial situation.

Agrihoods haven't just resuscitated Detroit from a state of dereliction and despair. They might have also created a blueprint for us all to use.

Because if you want my opinion, agrihoods are the future.

"Sustainable development is the pathway to the future we want for all. It offers a framework to generate economic growth, achieve social justice, exercise environmental stewardship and strengthen governance. "

– Ban Ki-moon, Politician and former United Nations Secretary-General.

#howonearth

PART III

#selfcare

(I only heard of this term 3 years ago and if you saw my nails that would probably come as no surprise. Self-care for me is putting on a face mask but it can be anything that makes you feel good.)

"What you do makes a difference, and you have to decide what kind of difference you want to make."

– Jane Goodall. Primatologist and Anthropologist.

#howonearth

The beauty industry is a billion-dollar business built on false promises that prey on our insecurities.

I used to waste all my hard-earned cash on fancy creams in nice bottles. It was only when I started reading the ingredients labels that I began to shun conventional products.

I discovered that everything you need for your skin is right there in your kitchen, and it costs pennies.

By ditching a hell of a lot of plastic packaging and a ton of nasty chemicals, I saved myself a small fortune too.

Companies charge an arm and a leg for products labelled organic, whether it's food, makeup, clothing, or cleaning supplies. The price is inflated by 200% just for displaying the precious O word.

Organic labeling causes product prices to go up, while still obscuring whether items are completely organic. This forces us to read the small print on the back of the label because simply being labelled as organic or natural doesn't mean it's completely free of chemicals.

We keep buying these products, so companies keep churning them out. It was so exhausting constantly reading all the labels, with the teeny, tiny print, coupled with my very limited budget. Finally, I gave up and started making my own products.

"Never doubt that a small group of thoughtful, committed citizens can change the world. Indeed, it's the only thing that ever has."

**– Margaret Mead
Cultural Anthropologist and Novelist.**

#howonearth

#skincare

(the skin is the body's largest organ. There's no point eating healthily if we're smothering ourselves in creams filled with toxins and wearing clothes manufactured with chemicals.)

"For the first time in the history of the world,
every human being is now subjected to contact
with dangerous chemicals, from the moment of
conception until death".

– Rachel Carson. Marine Biologist.

#howonearth

Honey is runny, gooey, marvellousness. It's the most natural antibacterial property produced on our planet.

It's so powerful it can be used to aide the most aggressive of skin conditions as it has an extremely low ph of 3.5. I've been using sugar and honey as an exfoliator for years now, long before microbeads were banned.

There are an estimated 330,000 microbeads in every face scrub. Microbeads, as well as being utterly dreadful for the environment, are also utterly dreadful at exfoliating your skin. For years we've been using little plastic balls, to scrub ourselves, when all the while we've had an abundance of sugar right in front of us.

Some blogs recommend using manuka honey or raw honey. But those products are pretty expensive, and, in all honesty, when I have bought them I couldn't tell the bloody difference anyway.

I just use bog-standard organic honey and some organic sugar, then mix the two into a paste in a bowl. It's organic, it's plastic-free, and it's readily available to all of us.

Turmeric is reportedly the most powerful herb on our planet. The benefits of using it on your skin include reducing dark circles, helping combat acne, and reducing blemishes and scars.

You need three things for a face mask: turmeric, egg white and tissue paper.

I do this once a month and it barely costs me anything. I don't even have to forward plan because I always have these things lying around in the kitchen. This mask will basically turn you into a bright orange, walking, talking, piece of papier- mache. When the mask has dried you can rip it off.

It's highly plausible that my sex life is slightly lacklustre at the moment. But, with that being said, nothing gives me greater satisfaction than tearing that face mask off and seeing all the crap it's pulled out of my pores.

1. Mix a pinch of turmeric with an egg white to make a paste.

2. Take one piece of tissue and tear it into strips.

3. Blow on the strips to separate the plys.

4. Spread the turmeric mixture on one area of your face with a sponge. I always start with the right cheek. Not sure why but it's as good a place as any.

5. Then add another piece of toilet paper and another layer of the mixture and repeat.

* beware that turmeric can leave your skin with an orange tinge so it's best not to do this right before you go out. I found that out the hard way so I'm just sharing the love over here.

Failing that, if all of the above sounds like too much of a faff on, lathering your face in natural yoghurt is absolutely mega. Simply wash your face, pat dry and then smother yourself in yoghurt. This is a great one if you're in a rush or, if like me, you need to use up your yoghurt before it starts to sprout penicillin at the back of the fridge. The lactic acid in yoghurt removes dead skin cells and leaves your skin glowing and looking fresh AF.

Yoghurt is honestly one of the best things I've ever used on my skin. It astounds me at how much brighter my skin is every time I use it.

We've been well and truly hoodwinked by the beauty industry when you think about it.

There are an estimated 723,000 of us who use face scrubs or face masks every single day.

If we each use 2 tubs of this per month. That's over 1.5 million plastic tubs going into landfill every four weeks.

If we all switch up the stuff we use on our faces we can save over 17 million plastic containers from going to landfills just from that one change.

Don't kid yourself that those plastic containers are recycled. Plastic has to be super clean to be recycled and those containers for face scrubs, face masks, toothpaste, etc. are utterly impossible to clean.

Apple cider vinegar is basically a miracle worker on your skin. Mix one part water and one part vinegar and you've got yourself a cheap as hell toner that balances your skin's PH levels.

If you have sensitive skin then just use more water or vice versa with problem skin. I tend to use more vinegar, as I have pretty hardy skin. I've often joked if I were a horse I'd be a shetland pony.

So, if my skin is having a nervous breakdown, which it tends to once a month, I'll just go hardcore with the Apple cider vinegar and dab the pure stuff over my face. When I wake up in the morning, my blemishes are basically gone.

If Apple cider vinegar does such a great job, why on earth was I using Benzoyl Peroxide on my blemishes for years?

Our skin is the largest organ of our body. Benzoyl Peroxide, in addition to being an industrial chemical used in the food and plastics industry, is also one of the most commonly prescribed treatments for acne.

Although it's been deemed safe for human use, when I actually thought about it, I realised it wasn't something I wanted to willfully slather on my face.

How have we honestly got to the point where we're willingly using industrial chemicals to cure our skin conditions?

"The plastic we throw away in a single year could circle the earth four times."

– Lucy Siegle. Environmental Journalist.

#howonearth

#smellyalater

(unsurprisingly there aren't many posts out there on the subject of smelling nice. So I'm using this one which has almost 34,000 posts, none of which are about our bodily scents.)

"There is no such thing as 'away'. When we throw anything away, it must go somewhere."

– Annie Leonard. Executive Director, Greenpeace USA

#howonearth

In my opinion, shower gel is potentially the world's biggest con. It will not only take your soul, but it will also take all of your hard-earned cash.

As of December 2017, the liquid soap market was worth a cool £365m.

Us humans go to great lengths to smell nice but I stopped using shower gel years ago purely because I decided it was a waste of money.

The alternative was to go back to a staple of my childhood, a good old fashioned bar of soap.

A bar of soap costs around £1.00, lasts a good few months and is typically made from fats and oils as opposed to man-made chemicals.

Because although shower gel may smell like a midsummer night's dream, it is in fact made using a ton of weird chemicals.

And the majority of shower gel brands in supermarkets do not offer any type of refill, so that's a hell of a lot of plastic we're using every single day just to smell fruity for the school run.

"Realise the political power of your money and spend it with the brands you know are treating their workers and the environment in the best possible way."

– Lily Cole, Model and Entrepreneur

#howonearth

#safetyrazor

(my Mum still has my Grandad's old safety razor. It's almost a hundred years old. I've probably spent more money on shaving in the last 20 years than my Grandad spent in his entire lifetime.)

"We're running the most dangerous experiment in history right now which is to see how much Carbon Dioxide the atmosphere can handle before it's too late"

– Elon Musk, Engineer and Entrepreneur

#howonearth

Apart from the odd eyebrow, I've never been one for waxing, instead choosing the trusty razor as my choice of hair removal. But those evil little things aren't recyclable and are, by far, the most wasteful product in your bathroom.

We're going through millions of them every single year and not only are they going to landfill, but it's estimated around 32% of them end up in the ocean.

Many millennials are embracing the no-shave movement but personally I like the feel of my fleece-lined pyjama bottoms against my fur-free legs.

So how do I do it?

With my trusty safety razor of course. And guess how often I'll have to replace it?

Well, the answer is never.

These fabulous shiny silver things should last you a lifetime. The thing that does need replacing is the blade, roughly once every two months. 50 blades will cost you around £20, which should last you around 9 years. The blades are 100% stainless steel which means that not only are they 100% recyclable they're also infinitely recyclable.

I read some horror stories online when I first bought this. But don't be alarmed. I am by no means a master when it comes to the art of shaving. So if I can use this thing without severing an artery, anyone can.

The next section is about feminine hygiene. If this section doesn't apply to you then you can just skip to page 171

#periodpower

"Water and air, the two essential fluids on which all life depends, have become global garbage cans."

– **Jacques Yves Cousteau, Explorer, Innovator, Conservationist.**

#howonearth

Growing up in a seaside town in the North of England we existed on fish and chips at least four days a week, there was always a stick of rock (that's pure sugar FYI) lying around, and the school holidays would be spent splashing around in the Irish sea, doing our best Klinsmann's* off the breakwater. All very idyllic until every once in a while we noticed a sanitary towel bobbing past us.

Back then, it was as common seeing a sanitary product on the beach as it was seeing a jellyfish. The fact we've grown up healthy after that is defying the majority of the laws of modern science. Thankfully, Lancashire County Council have since managed to up their sewer system game. Unfortunately the same can't be said for every corner of the planet. The correct disposal of feminine hygiene products is still an ongoing issue in the majority of countries around the world.

* a german footballer infamous amongst English football fans for his dramatic dives on the pitch.

We use an estimated 11,400 tampons in our lifetime. Besides the waste this creates, there's also the cost to consider. The average woman will spend around £18,000 throughout her life on period-related products.

My choice of feminine hygiene for a number of years was the trusty tampon.

Tampons are made from Viscose Rayon which is a synthetic fibre. Synthetic anything is always the devil.

This comes from wood pulp and is bleached before being mixed with cotton. The cotton is grown, sometimes using harmful pesticides before being moulded into the shape of a small sausage so that we can easily insert it into our vaginas.

The vagina is not only more sensitive but is also estimated to be 10 times more absorbent than the rest of our skin. So whatever is on that tampon seeps straight into our bloodstream. Yet we have no qualms about internally inserting something up there every single month of our lives.

If we use 11,400 tampons in our lifetime that's also 11,400 times we're exposing our body to the toxins in those tampons. For some crazy reason, there is very little research on the side effects of the absorption of chemicals from the cotton used in our tampons but we'd be very naive to think this has no effect whatsoever.

I actually bought my first menstrual cup back in 2014 after a recommendation from a friend, but it took me 12 months to start using it. Living in London I, like many other people, was disconnected from nature. I didn't really think about where anything went and would happily flush my tampons down the toilet every month without a care in the world.

But in 2015 I left London and did what everyone should do when they find themselves single and approaching their 30th birthday. I ran off to Portugal to live off-grid in the mountains for two months. It was without a shadow of doubt one of the best things I ever did because it was a real wake up call to how much waste we are generating in our day to day lives. I realised, that just because we put something in the bin doesn't mean it just disappears.

I like the cup because I'm pretty active and I spend a lot of time outdoors so it suits my lifestyle. But it really is exactly what its name says, a cup. A cup that collects the menstrual blood inside you. I know this isn't for everyone. My cousin faints at the sight of blood so it's certainly a no go option for her.

Another big motivator for the cup was the fact that it lasts 5 years. This year will be 5th year without conventional sanitary products. This means by the end of the year I'll have saved about 1,800 tampons from going down the toilet.

If the cup is not for you then you generally have two other options, free bleeding or sanitary pads.

I'm honestly so against sanitary pads. I think they're archaic and restrictive.

I personally think we should have a better option than this in the 21st century, but I also understand that for some people this is their preferred choice.

Reusable cloth pads are available from many internet sites. They're breathable, devoid of nasty chemicals, plastic-free and environmentally friendly.

Sanitary pads, although deemed safer than tampons due to the fact they work externally of the body still pose many health risks. They contain a number of chemicals, that are still in constant contact with the body causing irritations, and can also contain as much plastic as four plastic bags.

Sanitary waste is just one more contribution to the problem of waste disposal in developing countries, these countries will often burn their waste due to a lack of infrastructure regarding waste disposal.

 This releases toxic fumes along with CO_2. Although CO_2 is a naturally occurring gas, it's not something we want too much of. Just one molecule of CO_2 stays in the earth's atmosphere for an entire century. There are already enough of us breathing on this planet without us burning waste and adding to that problem.

I assumed period pants must be like incontinence pants when I first heard about these. But these are not just any old pants.

As knickers go, they're the Tesla of the undergarment industry. Harnessing new technology to eradicate the stigma around our monthly bleed and reducing plastic pollution in the process.

The gusset on these pants can hold around two tampons worth of blood whilst looking and feeling like a regular pair of pants.

They should actually be called magic pants.

If the thought of the cup weirds you out, or it's just not suitable for one reason or another, and you don't fancy reusable pads, then this is the route for you.

And whilst we're hovering around this glamourous topic, let's think about what we are wiping our nether regions with.

Global toilet paper production results in 27,000 trees being chopped down every single day.

It was only when I read that fact, that I actually began to question our method of wiping our bits.

Surely there must be a better way?

"If we could build an economy that would use things rather than use them up, we could build a future."

– Ellen Macarthur. Sailor and Founder of the Ellen Macarthur Foundation.

#howonearth

#bogroll

(If the panic buying of loo roll during the 2020 pandemic made us question anything it should be; do we really even need it!?)

"Destroying rainforests for economic gain is like
burning a Renaissance painting to cook a meal."

– EO Wilson, Biologist and Writer

#howonearth

If you've been to Asia, you'll know that the bum gun* is alive and well and doing a jolly good job of limiting toilet paper consumption. And if you've been to Spain on your jollies, you'll know that the bidet was also fairing rather well over there. But neither of these has ever taken off in the UK. I can only assume it's to do with the weather.

We blame the weather for everything else so why not this?

Except it's a pretty fair point that you don't want to blast cold water over your bits when it's minus five outside.

* the bum gun is a hand held bidet shower that allows you to clean yourself after defecation or urination.

I vividly remember being in the bathroom with my childhood best friend. We must have been around 3 or 4 years old when she proudly told me not to worry if there was ever a moment where there was no toilet paper, we could just use the hand towel instead. Aren't children precious? But in hindsight, she might just have been on to something.

The way it works is that you keep a box of the cloths in your bathroom, use them to wipe and then pop them in a hamper to be washed. Is this concept really so out there? It's really not that much different from the handkerchief.

But if I'm going to be honest, when I heard about this I recoiled in utter horror. I have a multitude of visual images of the stuff that goes on my toilet paper and suffice to say I'm pretty pleased that I can flush that away.

But the reusable toilet paper movement is a growing one, and I must hasten to add is generally only limited to number ones rather than number twos, which is something I didn't realise at first.

It's typically known as 'the family cloth' and I think if this needs to be widely adopted by the average joe then the first thing that has to go is that name.

It's estimated that the average UK family spends around £45 per year on loo roll. I actually think this must be way more if you're a twenty-something living in a shared house. I used to wonder if my housemates were using it for crocheting, judging by the rate at which we went through it.

"The climate crisis has already been solved. We already have the facts and solutions. All we have to do is wake up and change."

– Greta Thunberg. Environmental Activist

#howonearth

#EaudeBO

(I made this one up as I noticed there was somewhat of a drought on social media for hashtags regarding personal hygiene.)

"Imagine if trees gave off wifi signals. We would be planting so many trees and we'd probably save the planet too. Too bad they only produce the oxygen we breathe."

– Tarun Sarathe

#howonearth

I started to make the switch from conventional deodorant around 6 years ago. I went to my local organic shop and bought myself a very expensive organic roll-on deodorant. Within a few days, to my absolute horror, my entire underarm had developed an itchy rash. Not only that but my armpit smelt like a 20 bag of skunk*. The skin under my arm was pink and patchy and bore a slight resemblance to a Battenberg. Not the best look when you want to do some fist-pumping on the dancefloor on a Saturday night.

Unbeknownst to me, I was not alone. In fact, the majority of the friends I've spoken to about this over the last few years have all had the exact same problem. And these deodorants are not even remotely cheap. We're splashing out on them, only to use them once before rendering them useless and kicking them to the curb. That's not exactly eco-friendly.

* a bag of marijuana costing the sum of twenty English pounds.

So, I started off trying to make my own deodorant. Obviously it was an absolute disaster. There's a classic recipe using coconut oil, baking soda and an essential oil of your choice. The only essential oil I had to hand at that time was geranium oil. Have you ever smelt a geranium? If you could sum up the scent in one word it'd be 'musty'.

And have you ever met anyone that willingly wants their armpits to smell musty? No, me neither.

I smelt absolutely disgusting and quickly decided the process was too labour intensive for me. I just couldn't be bothered with it.

So I promptly went back to my old roll-on deodorant which was made with an abundance of hideous chemicals but smelt like an English country garden on a crisp autumn morning.

Fast forward 3 years and it's 2018. I'd started to try and reduce my personal plastic consumption and I was hunting for a deodorant that didn't come in plastic packaging.

And that was when I heard about the lemon.

Surely the humble lemon could not combat the smell emitted from my armpits during the 90% humidity I endure on my bicycle in the Far East?

Well, actually it can. I was beyond skeptical. In fact, I refused to believe it would work. I actually bought a lemon on my way home, and the next morning I sliced it in half, rubbed it under my arms and tepidly hopped on my bicycle with a slither of hope in my heart.

I assumed, that by the time I arrived at my destination I'd be smelling not too dissimilar to a nightclub when the smoking ban came into effect. If you're too young to remember this fabulous transition it was a scent that resembled something between half an onion and crusty old football socks.

But how wrong I was. Granted, I didn't smell like an English country garden, but I didn't smell of anything at all. I discovered that's because lemons are super acidic and the acid renders your pits uninhabitable for body odor. Why are we paying £8 for organic deodorants that don't work when there's a perfectly good one for 30 pence sitting right in front of us?

I'd spent hours hunting high and low for a deodorant with the least amount of chemicals with eco friendly packaging that didn't cost an arm and a leg and the whole time it was sat in the fruit shop across the road from my apartment.

Since chatting to people on instagram, I know that some people juice the lemon and put it in a spray bottle. Although it does make the lemon go further, I personally find the juice goes a bit sticky.

Also, I want whatever method is easiest for me so chances are if I have to remember to juice a lemon once a week I won't do it.

So I chop my lemon in half and use it that way.
I keep it on a shelf in the fridge which is easy for me since I live alone with my dog who exhibits very little interest in lemons. But I understand if you live with friends or a significant other then this might not be so simple.

If there's a very real possibility that the lemon is going to end up in someone's gin and tonic of a Friday evening then you need to figure out some sort of system.

Writing Eau de BO on the side of your Tupperware should probably ensure nobody goes near it.

"The earth is what we all have in common."

**– Wendell Berry. Poet, Novelist
and Environmental Activist.**

#howonearth

#bethechange

(If not us then who?)

Being eco-friendly, being more harmonious with nature, or just not being a dickhead, whatever you want to call it, it's a learning curve. Not just for me, or you, but for the whole world.

We're all changing our habits, and the only way to do that is to do it together.

All 7.5 billion of us, that's quite some team. But we're a team nonetheless. And regardless of our age, race, colour or creed, we all have one thing in common. And that's the fact that we all (hopefully) call Earth our home.

And if we continue to sit back and let climate change take hold, it won't matter who's Prime Minister, how good the camera is on the iPhone 11, or what this season's Pantone colour is. We're all going to be up the creek without a paddle.

As our world stands at this very moment in time, none of us can ever really be totally sustainable. Not one of us is perfect, regardless of what your social media feed leads you to believe.

Unless you're living a life of solitude, marooned up a mountain devoid of a smartphone, traveling on horseback and conjuring up a batch of goats cheese with your own fair hand every morning then I'm sorry, but your lifestyle isn't sustainable

And really, who honestly wants to live like that? We need to be progressing, not going back to the dark ages.

Despite the fact our lives can't be completely sustainable we can all take a step in the right direction. And like I said in the beginning, these are just some of the ways I do things.

It's by no means a comprehensive or universal list. And I don't have all the answers. I don't even think David Attenborough has all the answers.

But looking around at the world, from the most common everyday habits we have, to the complex industrial processes, you can see that we're doing it all wrong.

Everything we touch is tainted and it's time for that to change.

The future is in our hands. Some people might find that daunting, but I happen to think it's rather exciting.

Is it too little too late?

Who knows….

all we can do is try.

Afterword

If you want to see some pictures of my dog or some videos of me talking about environmental stuff you can follow me on Instagram @lianne_bell

And if you have a spare 15 seconds I will love you forever if you could please leave me a review on amazon, or post a pic of the book on your social media with #howonearth.

This book is completely self-published and self funded so any help from you is a huge help for us indie writers.

I hope you've enjoyed reading the book and I hope there's something here that you found useful.

I wrote this because I wanted to help people to see that being a bit more eco-friendly doesn't have to be daunting or overwhelming and it doesn't have to cost you a fortune.

Even if after reading this you still don't know where to start,.....

Please just buy less shit, eat more plants and celebrate your wears.

#educateandinspire

(We don't need no education………..
actually we do and learning is fun)

Further reading and research

Facebook groups

Thrifty Mutha Cookas

My friend Emily runs this group. People share their ideas or ask you for your ideas for making meals with the food that is lurking in the fridge. People conjure up some amazing concoctions without even setting foot in a shop.

Journey to zero-waste

Check out this global tribe of people trying to minimize their day-to-day waste. A great community for those starting out on their eco-friendly journey.

Zero Waste, Zero Judgement.

I like the ethos of this group. It's something I've talked about in this book. Judging one another will not get us anywhere. None of us are perfect, myself included, so get some team spirit in your life.

Further reading and research

Instagram

@maxlamanna

The original zero waste chef. Max's insta account is full of great plant-based ideas to minimize your food waste.

@emsladeedmonson

Emma is basically the secondhand shopping queen. Her episodes of 'come secondhand shopping with me' over on IGTV are absolutely awesome.

@zerowasteguy

Jonathan is a Project Manager in the waste management industry in LA. It's good to get a look inside recycling facilities since they're not somewhere the rest of us normally hang out.

Further reading and research

Instagram

@sophiebenson

I've been a big fan of Sophie's writing on sustainable fashion for a number of years now and her insta is filled with fabulous outfits which are all ethical or secondhand.

@_tidyguy

His Instagram content is immaculate, I feel like a grubby mess just looking at it but Tidy Guy shares some great zero waste tips.

@venetiafalconer

I only recently started following Venetia. I generally spend most of my time drooling over her amazing (and sustainable) outfits but I also like the fact she is not afraid to call herself out. None of us are perfect Venetia. Hooray for hypocrites.

Further reading and research

Instagram

@robjgreenfield
Rob is a sustainability activist and he is always bopping off on adventures. His posts are always out in nature and everything is so green, it's very inspiring and makes me want to get outdoors.

@amirah.and.dadas.garden
I love following this family and what they get up to in their garden. They have a small, very well looked after garden and it's very inspiring. You don't have to have an acre of land to grow your own vegetables.

@visiblemend
Kate Sekules could inspire even the most useless of us to pick up a needle and thread. Her feed is filled with beautiful needlework.

Further reading and research

Instagram

@ajabarber
Aja can be found on Instagram asking and addressing some really interesting questions surrounding intersectional feminism, racism and sustainability. I love her posts.

@shelterkingscross
This is a boutique charity shop designed by Wayne Hemingway, it probably has the best collection of secondhand clothes in the whole of the UK and they are not afraid to show it off.

@intotheeco
I love Lottie's posts and she's a bit of a globe trotter like myself. Wherever she is in the world she's always doing something interesting related to fashion and sustainability.

Further reading and research

Instagram

@girlwithbellsandwhistles
Kirsty shares the most fabulous secondhand outfits and some of the stuff she finds is sensational.

@lizzie_outside
Aside from being an all-round legend on the gram, Lizzie is also the founder of the community clean up app, Plastic Patrol.

@celinecelines
Celine Semaan runs the slow factory (@theslowfactory) which is a foundation offering education on environmental and social issues.

Further reading and research

Podcasts

Wardrobe Crisis

Clare Press is the Sustainability Editor of Vogue Australia and a fellow white wine fan. In this podcast, Clare chats to a ton of different people in the fashion industry about the various environmental impacts of our clothing.

The Minimalists

Joshua Fields Millburn and Ryan Nicodemus aka The Minimalists chat about living with less in this entertaining and informative podcast.

Further reading and research

Documentaries

True Cost

I sat my Mum down to watch this documentary about 5 years ago and she cried the whole way through. It's true that it's a tear-jerker in some parts but it displays the way our clothing is made in its rawest form. It's something we should all see.

River Blue

This documentary looks at the effects the fashion industry has had on different rivers around the world. It's a real eye-opener.

Cowspiracy

Still as relevant now as when it was first released 6 years ago. The environmental impact of animal agriculture is mind-blowing. Plus It's produced by Leonardo Di Caprio so you know it's not going to be total turd.

References

Barnes, Liz, and Gaynor Lea-Greenwood. "Fast Fashion: A Second Special Issue." *Journal of Fashion Marketing and Management: An International Journal*, vol. 17, no. 2, 3 May 2013, 10.1108/jfmm.2013.28417baa.001.

BBC: The Price of Fast Fashion. "BBC: The Price of Fast Fashion." *YouTube*, 2 Aug. 2019, youtu.be/GprVaAVPEI8. Accessed 27 Jan. 2020.

Bearne, Suzanne. "Manufacturing a New UK Clothing Industry." *Drapers*, 2018, www.drapersonline.com/business-operations/supply-chain/manufacturing-a-new-uk-clothing-industry/7031835.article.

Benson, Sophie. "One & Done: Why Do People Ditch Their Clothes After Just One Wear?" *Refinery29.Com*, Refinery29, 3 Oct. 2019, www.refinery29.com/en-gb/instagram-outfits-wear-once. Accessed 5 Nov. 2019.

Black, Sandy. *The Sustainable Fashion Handbook*. New York ; London, Thames & Hudson, 2013.

Carter, Rita, and Christopher D Frith. *Mapping the Mind*. Berkeley, University Of California Press, 2010.

Clive Humby, et al. *Scoring Points : How Tesco Continues to Win Customer Loyalty*. London, Koganpage, 2015.

Coley, David, et al. "Local Food, Food Miles and Carbon Emissions: A Comparison of Farm Shop and Mass Distribution Approaches." *Food Policy*, vol. 34, no. 2, Apr. 2009, pp. 150–155, getmoreeducation.org/Content/Modules/Module1/1_Coley_Howard_and_Winter_Food_Miles.pdf, 10.1016/j.foodpol.2008.11.001. Accessed 5 Nov. 2019.

de Haan, Peter, and Mario Keller. "Emission Factors for Passenger Cars: Application of Instantaneous Emission Modeling." *Atmospheric Environment*, vol. 34, no. 27, Jan. 2000, pp. 4629–4638, 10.1016/s1352-2310(00)00233-8. Accessed 13 Feb. 2019.

DW Documentary, The world's most polluted river. "The World's Most Polluted River | DW Documentary." *YouTube*, 25 Jan. 2020, youtu.be/GEHOlmcJAEk. Accessed 27 Jan. 2020.

Fearnley-Whittingstall, Hugh. "Hugh Fearnley-Whittingstall Takes on the Supermarket Giants | Hugh's War on Waste." *YouTube*, 27 Sept. 2019, youtu.be/v8gw-CioloE. Accessed 27 Jan. 2020.

Feloni, Richard. "Levi's Sees a Future in Hemp as a Sustainable Cotton Alternative - *Business Insider*." Business Insider, Business Insider, 24 Jan. 2020, www.businessinsider.com/levis-investing-in-hemp-as-a-cotton-alternative-2019-5. Accessed 27 Jan. 2020.

Fitzsimmons, Caitlin. "Second-Hand Clothing to Overtake Fast Fashion." *The Sydney Morning Herald*, The Sydney Morning Herald, 5 Oct. 2019, www.smh.com.au/business/consumer-affairs/second-hand-clothing-to-overtake-fast-fashion-20191004-p52xt4.html. Accessed 31 Oct. 2019.

Gustavsson, Jenny, et al. *Global Food Losses and Food Waste*. 2016.

Henson, Robert. The *Rough Guide to Climate Change*. London, Rough Guides, 2011.

Hickman, Martin. "Study Claims Meat Creates Half of All Greenhouse Gases." *The Independent*, 1 Nov. 2009, www. independent.co.uk/environment/climate-change/study-claims-meat-creates-half-of-all-greenhouse-gases-1812909.html.

ICF for EPA. *GUIDE TO SUSTAINABLE TRANSPORTATION PERFORMANCE MEASURES*. 2011.

Kozlowski, Anika, et al. "Environmental Impacts in the Fashion Industry." *Journal of Corporate Citizenship*, vol. 2012, no. 45, 1 Mar. 2012, pp. 16–36, 10.9774/gleaf.4700.2012.sp.00004.

Langley, Joseph, et al. "Food for Thought? — A UK Pilot Study Testing a Methodology for Compositional Domestic Food Waste Analysis." *Waste Management & Research*, vol. 28, no. 3, 26 May 2009, pp. 220–227, 10.1177/0734242x08095348. Accessed 5 July 2019.

Malaysia, in. "British Recycling Found Dumped in Malaysia." *YouTube*, 23 Oct. 2018, youtu.be/jpUplUHw4Dk. Accessed 27 Jan. 2020.

Nicole, Wendee. "A Question for Women's Health: Chemicals in Feminine Hygiene Products and Personal Lubricants." *Environmental Health Perspectives*, vol. 122, no. 3, Mar. 2014, www.ncbi.nlm.nih.gov/pmc/articles/PMC3948026/, 10.1289/ehp.122-a70. Accessed 13 Sept. 2019.

Pauli, Gunter A. Blue Economy 3.0 : *The Marriage of Science, Innovation and Entrepreneurship Creates a New Business Model That Transforms Society*. Gordon, Nsw]: Xlibris, 2017.

Pinnock, Olivia. "Sustainable Fashion Searches Surged In 2018." *Forbes*, 20 Nov. 2018, www.forbes.com/sites/oliviapinnock/2018/11/20/sustainable-fashion-searches-surged-in-2018/. Accessed 21 Oct. 2019.

Roberts-Islam, Brooke. "Second-Hand Is The Answer To Sustainable Fashion, Says Oxfam." *Forbes*, 1 Sept. 2019, www.forbes.com/sites/brookerobertsislam/2019/08/31/second-hand-is-the-answer-to-sustainable-fashion-says-oxfam/. Accessed 27 Jan. 2020.

Sara Jane Strickland. "It's Too Late for Ethical Fashion." *I-D*, i-d, 6 Sept. 2019, i-d.vice.com/en_us/article/mbmg4a/its-too-late-for-ethical-fashion. Accessed 27 Jan. 2020.

Siegle, Lucy. *To Die for : Is Fashion Wearing out the World ?*. London, Fourth Estate, 2011.

---. *TURNING THE TIDE ON PLASTIC : How Humanity (and You) Can Make Our Globe Clean Again*. Trapeze, 2019.

Simms, Andrew. *Tescopoly*. Constable, 2013.

Unravel: The final resting place of your cast-off clothing. "Unravel: The Final Resting Place of Your Cast-off Clothing." *YouTube*, 30 Nov. 2016, youtu.be/bOOI5LbQ9B8. Accessed 27 Jan. 2020.

Where, India: "India: Where Old Clothes Go to Get a New Life." *YouTube*, 29 Aug. 2017, youtu.be/_JZUOCsnQqY. Accessed 27 Jan. 2020.

978-1-5272-6109-9

Published by Lianne Bell
www.liannebell.com

Printed in Great Britain
by Amazon

54504769R00127